Freedom for Flowers

The Secrets to Peace and Joy and Love Revealed by a Butterfly and Botanicals
by Casey Tennyson

INSIDE: Butterfly Cat searches for a spiritual promise to find Peace and Joy and Love. She also yearns to fulfill a dream to fly to The Sky. The botanicals she engages in her quest enlighten her about nature, and the nature of all living beings. She discovers that the concepts of Faith and Freedom are essential to both spiritual and worldly dreams.

AUTHOR: Casey Tennyson has used her writing skills as a leader in advertising, marketing, publishing and ghostwriting. Like many of her books, her sixth book "Freedom for Flowers" celebrates the human spirit and embraces the tender parts of humanity. Her books typically use settings in tropical Florida and the Caribbean where she taps into her creative energy, intuition and inspiration. Tennyson's own garden inspired "Freedom for Flowers".
Tennyson also is the publisher of Chart charity art magazine in Florida since 2005.

Praise for some other books by Casey Tennyson

CLEVER "'**Secrets of the Southern Shells**' is a very clever and original allegory containing much wisdom that has been passed down from Southern mothers to their daughters, the Southern Belles. This charming book, filled with very attractive marine artwork, relates a powerful story of sea creatures, and how one, a mere starfish, overcomes impossible obstacles and achieves her dreams because she faithfully heeds her mother's timeless advice. In seven words: Buy it, read it, and gift it!"
— Bill Guggenheim, co-author of bestseller "Hello From Heaven!"

A VIVID JOURNEY OF THE SENSES AND THE SOUL "I loved **'Catalyst in Palm Beach'**! Author Casey Tennyson takes the reader on a riveting adventure of the senses and the soul. The story takes us from jet-setting to Europe, to island-hopping through the Caribbean, with colorful characters and some sketchy creepers. Catalyst is a cautionary tale of balancing levity and awareness, and learning to be vigilant about what you allow into your reality. In today's world, we have to be critical thinkers when sifting through the news, political and religious ideologies, and the people whom we allow to be close to us. The protagonist, Cat, has an uncanny sense of being guided and protected, which allows her to be present and in-the-moment, even when danger and threats abound. As a psychotherapist, I know that many people struggle to achieve this balance. The story encourages the reader to adjust the lens through which we see things, and discover one's own truth. Full of life lessons, hair raising moments and incredible adventures, 'Catalyst in Palm Beach' is irresistible and eye-opening. As an avid reader, this is a story that will stay with me and remind me to live my best life, being guided by love and not fear."
– Risa Bos, LMHC

INSPIRATIONAL "I truly enjoyed reading **'Marlins Cry A Phishing Story.'** My very favorite line in the book is 'You have the protection of the wings of one thousand angels. Look up. Protecting them are one thousand more for every star of the sky.' Thank you for a very compelling, yet a bit scary, read. And thank you for that line of inspiration when some days life seems a bit too much to handle. LOVED IT."
— Tracie Sayyah

BIG BOOK OF LIFE

"'**Marlins Cry A Phishing Story**' is more than a slice of life. In a few succinct chapters this is a Big Book of Life. Each chapter has a novel-size volume of depth. The way the author creates a sequence of words of profound simple truths of humanity makes her a powerful, relevant voice of our time. The book reads as if you were in all the places, you were involved in the dramas, you were part of the scene and part of the very same life. What a voice for modern story telling weaving moments in time ... how words have power to express universal truths. The main character asks, 'What do you stand for and how do you live up to it?' Everyone knows the sharks, the alligators, characters but to understand the Marlin is big. I am going to read this book time and again for deeper meaning. I am an avid reader, and

when I read this book, I thought, '**This is a writer. Casey Tennyson can write.**'"

– Xenia Psihas

Galatians 6:7–9
reap what you sow

Title
Freedom for Flowers
The Secrets to Peace and Joy and Love Revealed by a Butterfly and Botanicals

Author and Photographer
Casey Tennyson

International Standard Book Number
ISBN number 978-0-9855264-4-3

Published in the USA Sept. 2023
Written Labor Day Weekend as a Labor of Love
to write an allegory about The American Dream
and
Published Sept. 11, 2023
in remembrance of 9/11 (2001) in NYC
and in gratitude for our Freedoms

Photos and a Photo Credit
The untouched photos reveal the perfectly pleasant imperfections of nature.
Butterflies flutter all around the botanicals, but busy butterflies are difficult to photograph.
Many thanks to Kim Knight for sharing her photo of Monarch butterflies.

Author's Preface

PREFACE

Per instructions, I wore bright colors for my friend Bill's Celebration of Life on July 16, 2023 at Leu Gardens. Bill (William Guggenheim III) lived from Mar. 2, 1939 to May 20, 2023 and transitioned at 84-years-old.

I missed Bill. But, of course I would miss Bill. It was predictive in his own words that I put in my book "Catalyst in Palm Beach" just why I would miss him so.

Over several decades of friendship, Bill was my confidant. I didn't actually have to disclose anything at all. He was highly spiritual and incredibly intuitive so when we would meet or talk on the phone he would read me like a book. He would give light advice, warnings and affirmations. He told me I would have five leaks in my house for example, and a month later, I did. He was a gentle kind generous soul who offered ongoing encouragement for my writing. He was a best-selling co-author of "Hello From Heaven!" about After Death Communication or ADC. He was particularly supportive of my efforts as an author and filmmaker.

I found my handwritten notes from the mid 1990s of a conversation with Bill about how he perceived me. At the time I was interviewing happily married friends for a gift book titled, "Picket Fences." Bill was encouraging of my endeavor and of me in general. I put part of my conversation with Bill in as fiction in my novel "Catalyst in Palm Beach."

EDITED EXCERPT is below where in this conversation I was the real character Cat and the real Bill responded as the fictional character J in my book "Catalyst in Palm Beach."

"My next man has to have a last name beginning with M. My initials when I married became 'CATS' and I intend for my next four marriages to spell 'MEOW' so my epitaph will be 'CATS MEOW,'" I grinned.

"Your words are silly but your heart is serious. You have a very strong personality, a born leader. You push men to the edge, just to see how they will react. Then you push them over, just for curiosity, not to be mean. You are surrounded by men. They are like flowers to you. You like to see how they smell. But you need time to yourself. Writing is a lonely profession. You find you are happy by yourself. But your longing for love lingers. You find peace around the water, you like boating, sailing, travel, and romance. Find a man who enjoys the same things and quit being afraid to commit. You don't like committing in relationships because you are so deeply affected when it ends. It affects everyone but it takes you so long to heal. You have to understand that all things have a beginning and an end. Just like a plant. It's natural that it ended. Just because it ends, doesn't mean it was bad. It wasn't supposed to last. Your relationships didn't fail, they ended. You picked your husband and children before you were ever born for spiritual reasons. You attract successful men who are accustomed to controlling their surroundings. So, they control you, too. Then you rebel."

Bill was once again right in his insights on my life about being deeply affected when things end, in this case his absence in 2023.

In my spiritual reality, Bill wasn't absent at all. For birthdays he would bring a whole bag of individually wrapped thoughtful small gifts. After he transitioned, I sorted through things he had given me over the years, mostly books, and I noticed many were about flowers. I then recalled several decades ago Bill told me I was going to write a book about flowers. So, here I was in the sultry Summer of Stillness of 2023 puttering in my garden. The words began to flow for the flower book he predicted so many years earlier.

He gave high praise to my gift book "Secrets of the Southern Shells" about a starfish sharing 20 tips of a Southern mother's timeless wisdom. I decided to write a companion book in a garden setting.

The social butterfly visiting the flowers were all to offer gardening tips through the storyline. That is how the book started and then other concepts spilled into the characters and plot through the writing process. My interest in documenting The American Dream presented itself. In my own intuition (through God) I sensed a promise of peace and joy and love. The search for the steps to that promise led me to my quiet place and away from my IT-girl space. I put pen to paper and, as the botanicals and nature spoke to my creativity, the story unfolded.

RELATED WORKS BY THE AUTHOR

In my 2019 novel "Catalyst in Palm Beach" the chapter "Growing Guidance in Your Garden" suggests to get in nature for meditation and spiritual guidance. If you are not near a beach or mountains, take a few steps in nature close to you. Nature is a good reminder that all things evolve and that there is intrinsic beauty in every state of eternal change. Through the story line, the book offers tips and suggestions for developing your spiritual self to become more mindful and intuitive. The physical world around you possibly is more restrictive, while an inner spirit life will soothe and replenish you.

I also put in my 2019 novel "Catalyst in Palm Beach" a 2017 poem inspired by my garden.

"The Rest"

Pink camellias in my garden,
Azaleas in full fuchsia bloom,
In my head, I could be most anywhere,
Breathing with nature in my outside room.

A wide-winged majestic dragonfly
Fluttered from behind a palm.
A red cardinal keeping dutiful watch
Added to the realm of calm.

A crane pecked at a lizard.
A neighbor's cat napped with a purr.
Squirrels scampered around the mulch
Where sunflower seeds once were.

I walked and watered and puttered
And stood in amazement before the rose.
I am reminded of those before me
And how what one plants surely grows.

In my little space I wondered
What seeds that I shall sow.
And my gentle Voice inside me
Again urged the vision I was to go.

As I trimmed herbs in pots,
The fear welled up inside me.
And my Voice said, "Look to that above.
What is that placed upon the tree?"

On an outer branch above my door
A bird had constructed a massive nest.
"So you do your work as birds have done,
And I will do the rest."

"A promise was made for protection
With the soft whisper of a feather
Of the wings of one thousand angels.
Your work is blessed ... in any weather."

"And when you sense a drought
In your garden look to the sky.
And remember I am with you,
And with me, you will surely fly."

- Casey Tennyson April 24, 2017

Contents

You are
Free to
Create
The Dream

Freely Dream

   Once upon a time, a serene spiritual space overflowed with flora and fauna and shared the secrets of Peace and Joy and Love. Cat had been promised these things as her heart's desire by The Sky. She felt this promise deep in her soul, and it was her destiny to find it.

   Cat had been still and quiet for quite some time. She awoke to stimulating sensations. She had been cognizant of the warmth of The Sun's rays, but had not in a very long time witnessed the pre-dawn light glisten the dew over the garden. She had obediently followed every innate task to transition to a Butterfly. She had set her dreams high. Now, finally, she could fly to The Sky. That was her worldly dream, to fly to The Sky. She had earned her wings. She was a regal Monarch with both a promise from The Sky and a dream from her inner self. With a promise and a dream, anything was possible in Picket Park Place.

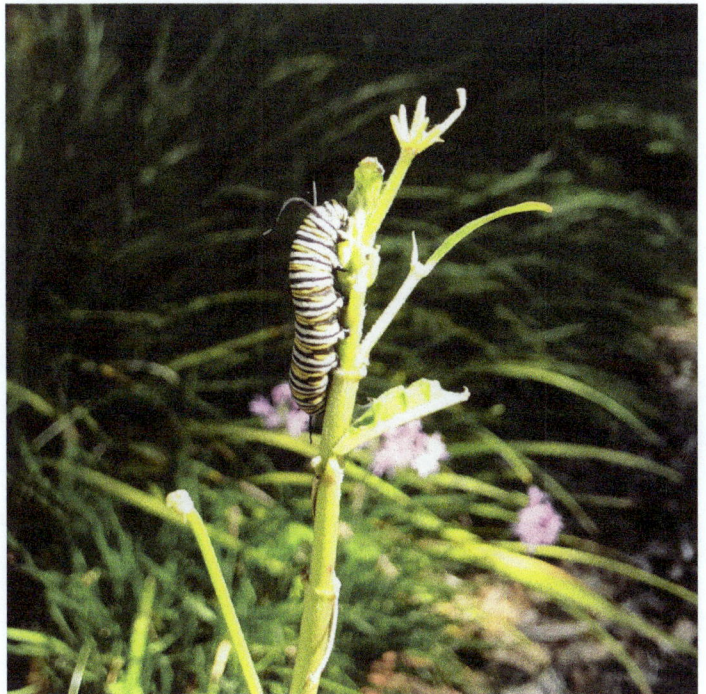

Photo: Milkweed or Butterfly Weed,
Asclepias Tuberosa

Make Room to Bloom

Cat's new perspective from flying over the enchanting lush gardens thrilled her. She flapped and floated and fluttered around the tops of the flowers. The fragrant lilac spheres of the Society Garlic blooms attracted Cat.

"Hi, my name is Cat. You all smell so spicy and invigorating this morning," Cat introduced herself and took a deep breath to savor their scent.

"You are a Butterfly, not a cat," stated the tallest of the Society Garlic clan.

"Oh, I indeed am not a cat. I was a caterpillar just a short while ago and now, yes, I am a proud Butterfly. I will keep my name Cat. I treasured my time as a Caterpillar so I am choosing to keep my name even though I have changed in appearance. I am most certainly still Cat inside. We don't ever fully change. We always bring our past into our present and inevitably into our future.," Cat explained herself.

"Well, we understand change. Just like the seasons, we have grown over the generations in different spaces since the beginning in Picket Park Place. The last few years we were clustered uncomfortably in two clay pots. One pot had too much water and the other pot had too little. Our roots were crowded together and we were in decline. We did not bloom. We were all but forgotten. Our plight was not noticed until we were once again needed as sun-loving plants. Now we resumed our status at the pinnacle of Picket blooming and thriving in our own individual spaces. Now our roots can grow and our stalks expand. We are blooming again," explained the local historian to the new Butterfly.

Cat said, "Blooming and beaming, you live in the greatest garden ever!"

Society Garlic explained further, "The Fall of The Great Oak happened last fall during The Great Wind Catastrophe. He epitomized our ideal of The Dream of Picket Park Place. He started as a tiny sapling and in time the whole gardens were planted around him as the focal point. He exemplified the ethos of our determined work ethic towards creating individual Beauty. Each of us bloomed and the garden burst with prosperity and pride. The Great Oak left smaller Oaks but he was the one that provided most of the shade and protection for Picket. After his demise, came a summer of drought and 100-year record-setting heat. The front plots were accustomed to shade from the massive tree. The Sun started bearing down and many plants got sun-burned and were dying. Society Garlics are now back in the front plot where we started and are thriving under The Sun. We needed the opportunity of more space. Now we have room to bloom. Some of us will survive."

Photo: Society Garlic, Tulbaghia Violacea, edible flowers and leaves

Cat curiously looked around and all the plants seemed to be healthy at first glance.

Society Garlic noted her gaze and continued, "Just because you do not see waning plant life does not mean that there was not great suffering. Catastrophes pass and life re-adjusts and re-builds itself. We now are where the Bromeliads bloomed. They touted grand spouts of regal red when they bloomed. Each plant bloomed just once in its lifetime, but they continually produced pups so the colorful band perpetually created splendid displays of Beauty. Everything in Picket revolves around ideal Beauty. Their delicate leaves were not suitable for direct sunlight so they shriveled under the heat and wrath of The Sun. They did not adapt in time. They didn't change, so they were changed. They disintegrated as we all watched with great sadness. A few pups were moved to a pot, just like we were moved to a pot before them during the long season of shade. Bromeliads can come back to the plot one day. It's possible. But they will have to wait for shade, much like we had to wait for The Sun. Everything is in perfect balance under The Sky. First we had the long era of shade, and now we will endure the season of The Sun."

Cat responded, "I remember the Bromeliads when I was a caterpillar. The friendly snails lived under them."

"They housed snails under them and bred mosquitoes in their cupped blooms. While nature under-stands that we all co-exist and have purpose, the hordes of snails and mosquitoes were not exactly welcome in Picket. When the Bromeliads perished, the others had to move. They were friendly with Bromeliads but not with others in Picket. They learned a good lesson to be neighborly. If they had other friends and allies, possibly they could have stayed," mentioned Society Garlic with a sigh.

"Why didn't the Bromeliads move in time to save themselves?" asked Cat.

"Indecisiveness in matters of sun or shade, light or dark, or good or evil, puts one in harm's way. De-lay could mean destruction. Any decision of critical importance should not be delayed. The Bromeliads didn't change, so nature changed life for them, and not for the best outcome. It's wise to choose a change. Choose change. Even if it's not the perfect decision in all ways, it's controlled by you," offered the elder.

Photo: Bromeliads, Bromeliaceae

Change or Be Changed

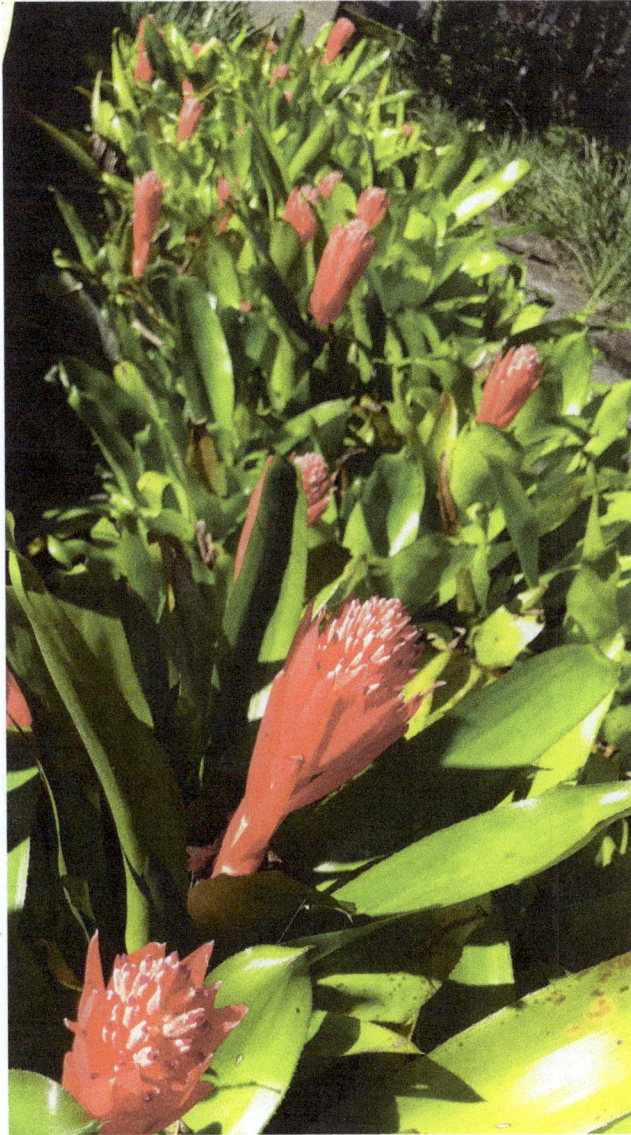

"Choose change."

Take Out the Takers

Cat was wondering compassionately if the snails passed away as a result of the Bromeliad fiasco. She hoped they had moved and were living safely elsewhere.

A Weed popped up from beside Society Garlic and interrupted the conversation, "Well, we Weeds, like the snails, are not welcome either, but here we make ourselves at home. We intentionally target neglected plots to spread and populate exponentially. When plots are re-planted with intended species, and the water and nutrients flow, our seeds are sown hidden beneath the soil to take over the area. Then we expand to all the connected areas. We can grow faster than most flowers and plants so we take what is theirs."

"That doesn't seem honorable," admonished Cat.

"We are not concerned with honor. We are the takers, the opportunists. We camouflage ourselves among the plants and mimic their behavior as pretenders, fakes and phonies. See, I am hiding here by the stem but note subtle differences such as my leaves grow thinner and taller than Society Garlic. Under the soil, I sip their water. I feast on their fertilizer. I rest on their roots. The Clover next to us blooms also in purple as an attempt to blend in then take from Society Garlic, too," explained the perpetrator.

"So, why don't you have your own area? How do the plants in Picket get you to move away?" asked Cat.

"Oh, please! Once we set in, we will never, ever leave. We only get bolder. The only way to avoid us is to destroy us," proclaimed Weed in a big, loud and proud voice.

Cat was taken aback by her aggression. Her brazen entitlement both confused and disgusted Cat. She had worked so diligently in her quest to fly to The Sky that she was dumbfounded by the notion of just taking what belongs to others instead of earning successes and blessings. Cat was not one to be combative but she was wondering what would Picket have to do to destroy Weed. This Weed and her sisters and friends were an obvious problem.

Society Garlic interceded, ignored Weed, and assured Cat, "We have taken out the takers before and we'll do it again. Weeds did not like the structure, rules and control of The Great Oak era so they stayed away or at least stayed hidden. Weeds sneak in when we are vulnerable. After the Fall of The Great Oak, The Sun shocked the plants of Picket and made us weaker until we could adjust. We are getting strong again. Weeds can't take root when our own sturdy roots cover our spaces. Their days are numbered in Picket. They have no loyalty on this land so their survivors will just move on, then try to cycle back at some point when they sense weakness. History teaches us that life happens in cycles. You can't reason with Weeds. You have to take out the takers."

Photo: Weeds hiding by Society Garlic, Tulbaghia Violacea, edible flowers and leaves

Protect Yourself

In the susurrus of Picket, Cat heard a "pssst" sound.

A Hydrangea was summoning her. She had browned leaves and was hunched over a bit. She bore one perky pink bloom but it seemed small for a Hydrangea.

"Be careful talking to or about Weeds. They are tricky, conniving and unethical. They falsely convinced the Oaks that the very tall Fishtail Palms, Bird of Paradise and Umbrella Trees were actually tall weeds because they had some brown growth on their tops high in the air. They got taken out of Picket. Their absence is a shame because now with The Great Oak gone, their shade would be most helpful. Some little ones of the alleged giant Weeds have popped up in their former places, but stay small, no taller than I am, so as not to bring attention to themselves so they don't get cut down again," warned Hydrangea.

"How do you know Weeds were at fault? Maybe there was a reason the tall ones were trimmed or removed or maybe they wanted to move," pondered Cat always trying to find the goodness in a situation.

"Shhh! Not so loud. We cannot speak of these things. They will hear you," said a seemingly paranoid and frightened Hydrangea.

"Who can hear me? And who cares? We are in Picket in the land of The Great Oak. We can speak freely of anything. You are being overly cautious it seems to me. I'm not saying you are wrong. Your opinion matters. I am listening and your warning I have noted, although I do not understand it fully," said Cat.

"Weeds have infiltered every plot. With our summer super-heat and the drought, the plants of Picket are struggling but Weeds can thrive on little nurturing so they are being quite brazen and obnoxious. Blight is taking over our Beauty," explained Hydrangea.

"Think pink! Pink power! Bloom big! Dig into your dignity! Make up your mind to grow bigger and even more beautiful. Drop your brown leaves and sprout new green growth. Push your roots deeper and wider. Bloom big pink puffs. If you are stealth and vibrant, there is no space for a Weed to get near to you. You can keep the Weeds away from you and from all of Picket. It is within the power of each plant to overcome Weeds near them. If every plant was thriving, Weeds would go elsewhere. Do what you must do. Get strong. Protect yourself," suggested Cat.

Photo: Hydrangea, Hydrangea Macrophylla

"Gratitude ignites growth."

Grow with Gratitude

Cat fluttered over to a smaller Oak near where The Great Oak had lived.

"I couldn't help but to hear you and Hydrangea. Picket is a small circle. Hydrangea is not meant for sunshine so she is not doing well and is trying to blame the Weeds. When we moved, the soil was moved around and sifted so we have very little Weeds around us. Moving is a good time to let go of things and make changes. The Weeds near her are certainly not helping matters but Hydrangea could have moved here like we did after the Fall of The Great Oak. Some of us simply do better in shade. The Sun is harsh with its lessons of nature and this summer sunshine is delivering severe consequences to plants of Picket. When things don't feel right, one has to make a move," said Ginger.

"That makes sense. You have to listen to the guidance of your inner voice and also Mother Nature's nudging. Hydrangea could also stay where she is but she has to make some sort of shift to get healthier. She is wilting. She no longer seems to reflect her Beauty," said Cat.

"I'm so grateful we moved under one of the smaller Oaks. At least we get some shade, not as much as before, but enough. None of us realized how much we depended upon the protection of The Great Oak. He protected us from The Sun, but also hard rains, hail, winds and other perils we likely did not even recognize. We take direct hits now from all kinds of foul subtropical weather. We now are so thankful for some protection under this smaller Oak. We are growing high like we were before The Fall of The Great Oak. We value progress over pristine conditions. We may have a few brown spots, but we are so thankful we are mostly green. Gratitude ignites growth," said Ginger.

Photo: Variegated Shell Ginger, Alpinia Zerumbet Variegata

Share Joy

Just outside of the shade of the smaller Oak, next to where The Great Oak had lived, a colorful cacophony of blooms enticed Cat with their cheerful banter. The Sun was searing more intensely as it rose splashing long shadows and sunrays across the landscape. The depth of shadows added to the natural elegance of Picket. Dark highlights light. Each has their purpose.

"Some of us simply shine under shade or sunlight," arrogantly bragged a Red Button Ginger.

"We love The Sun and The Sun loves us. We look even more gorgeous in the bright light. We are so colossal that we could actually be an Oak if we desired," exaggerated Hawaiian Ti.

"Red rates highest for aesthetics. Look at my athleticism. Look at these magnificent red clustered blooms. I attract the most bees, butterflies and hummingbirds of any of the others. I am simply irresistible," boasted a young Jatropha Tree with a little swagger move of his upper branches in the breeze.

"Who is buzzing? I think it is I that attracts the most bees of all. And I smell just divine. Sniff-sniff and Whiff-whiff. I smell wonderful," proudly gloated a blooming sweet basil herb buzzing with honey bees.

"Bees like us, too! Buzz-buzz-buzz! We pop with the most color. Purple and pinks are the prettiest," bragged the petite Pentas.

"We are pink, too! Pink is pretty! Pink is precious! Pink is perky! We also bloom white like cotton-ball clouds. Look at us! We are the loveliest of all," squealed the little Periwinkles.

Purslane opened her blooms after closing for nighttime, and seductively purred, "Notice my bright colors! Hot sexy flowers in hot pink on a hot day wins every time! I'm ornamental like all of you, but medicinal and edible, too!"

"You are all delightful and desirable. You individually are stunning and as a whole you create a flamboyant magical cohesive effect. How lucky you are to have each other! The joy you share with each other brought me joy today. Thank you for sharing your joy," excitedly exclaimed Cat.

Photo: Periwinkles in Pink, Vinca Flower, Catharanthus Roseus or Lochnera Rosea

Photo: Hawaiian Ti, Cordyline Fruticosa
Pentas, Pentas lanceolata
Jatropha Tree, Jatropha Integerrima
Red Button Ginger, Costus Woodsonii
Basil, Ocimum Basilicum, edible herb
Purslane, Portulaca Oleracea, medicinal
and edible

Share Joy

Be the Beauty

"The Pink Patch is so joyful and playful," Cat affirmed to herself as she flew over to savor the scents.

Pinwheel Jasmine was new to Picket and offered his opinion to Cat in a hushed tone, "Just listen to them self-aggrandizing. This cheery clique is so self-focused they don't care about the rest of the botanicals. They don't sincerely care about each other either. They just chatter all day amongst themselves about their physical Beauty."

"They are pretty. They seem pretty happy, too. I want to be joyful like them. I want to find joy. When I was a caterpillar, I was promised by The Sky that I would find Peace and Joy and Love," noted Cat and she asked, "Are you not happy here?"

"Their joy will not bring you joy. The experience of joy is as unique as each of the flowers themselves. They exude joy as a group. Joy is more noticeable and obvious when it is shared. I am joyful in a less conspicuous manner, and I am not always joyful. Joy is not a possession but a fleeting gift," he noted.

"They made me happy in the moment. Moments of joy can be strung together and make up a whole life. Being near their joy does not bring you joy?" asked Cat.

"I am content in some ways that I am in the gilded part of Picket but I get lonely for substance and yearn for higher-thinking. The little flowers look at me as antediluvian or excessively old-fashioned. I simply have a wider world-view so I see them as simpletons. I appear like a flower now but I will grow first into a bush and then into a small tree. My destiny is greater than the little ones surrounding me. I can only think about the colors pink and purple and red so many times in a day without growing bored. Beauty is a core value of Picket. I understand it's essential. Physical Beauty is pleasurable but not satisfying in and of itself. Outer Beauty alone is not fulfilling. Ideal Beauty can actually be a barrier to true fulfillment for some if they don't take the time to fully understand the idea behind it," he admitted.

She found him intellectual and interesting but with a whim of arrogance.

"I don't believe that one destiny is more important than another. We are all connected. You seem to have a wise sense about you so share your knowledge with the flowers so they, too, can become more worldly and well-rounded. Share your expertise and your visions of Beauty. Instead of being somber, be happy. You be the Beauty you want to see in the others," advised Cat.

Photo: Pinwheel Jasmine, Tabernaemontana Divaricata

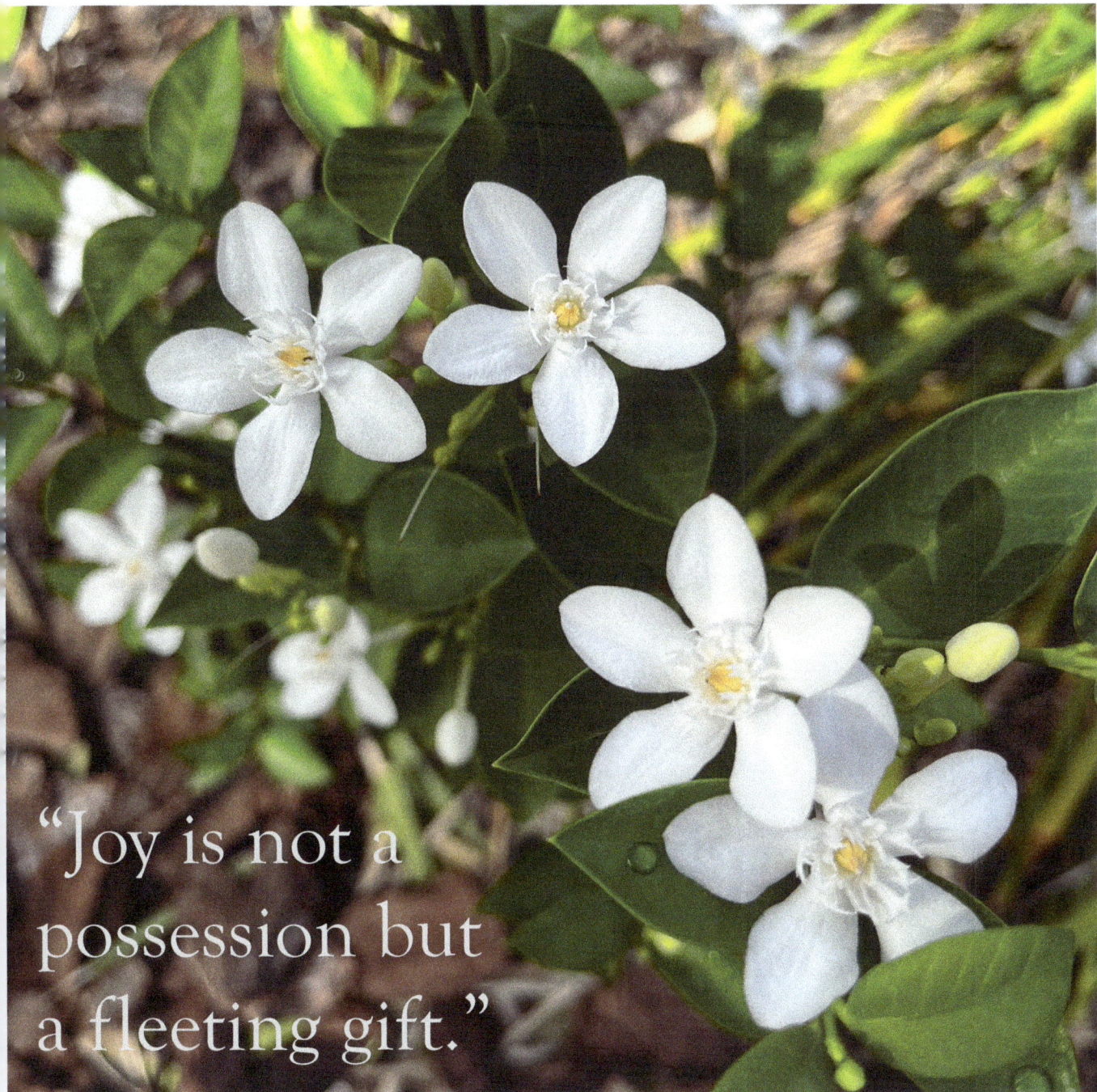

"Joy is not a
possession but
a fleeting gift."

Affirm Abundance

"Pink. Pink. Pink. I'm not sure why the Pinks get the most prestigious plot, when everyone knows blue is best," one-upped Plumbago.

"Blue me. Blue you. I'm blue, too! Blue is true!" excitedly exclaimed the miniature Blue Daze.

"I'm not sure any of you individually have more Beauty. You certainly bring out the best in each other. All the colors and shapes and sizes ... I find you all simply delightful," comforted Cat.

"We compete. It's true. We all want to be the most beautiful. We want the most. More, more, more! Beauty is the most valued virtue in Picket. We all work hard to earn it," pointedly said Plumbago.

"You are all most beautiful living together because you each contribute something unique and special to the whole shape, color and texture spectrum," suggested Cat.

"We have to boast. The underlying truth is that resources are lacking in Picket now, so we will not all prevail. Some of us will have to move again or worse," whispered Plumbago with a harsh annoyed tone.

"I believe in abundance. Don't you? Surely something will come from The Sky that provides for all of us," retorted Cat.

"You are very naive. Cute, but naive," said Plumbago dismissively and stopped talking to her altogether.

Little Blue Daze shrugged in the breeze.

Asparagus Fern stood silent and listened. He had learned that wise men sometimes say nothing at all.

Cat started flying away and said an affirmation to herself out loud knowing the others would hear. Others always hear. They may not listen but they will hear. They may listen in time. Listening is different than hearing.

"I believe in complete abundance and provision for all things under The Sky," affirmed Cat.

She looked back and saw Plumbago loosen his tense crossed branches. Dainty Blue Daze and pals were jumping up and down wtih glee and clapping in the wind. Asparagus Fern gave Blue Daze a pat on his top. They all were smiling. They did listen.

"We are the colors of The Sky! The Sky loves us! We reflect The Sky! Remember? Remember Plumbago? The Sky provides. The Sky protects. The Sky and I! Sky blue, me and you!" cheerily peeped Blue Daze.

Photo: Plumbago, Plumbago Auriculata
Blue Daze, Beach Bum Blue, Evolvulus Glomeratus
with Foxtail or Asparagus Fern, Asparagus Setaceus

"I believe in complete abundance and provision for all things under The Sky."

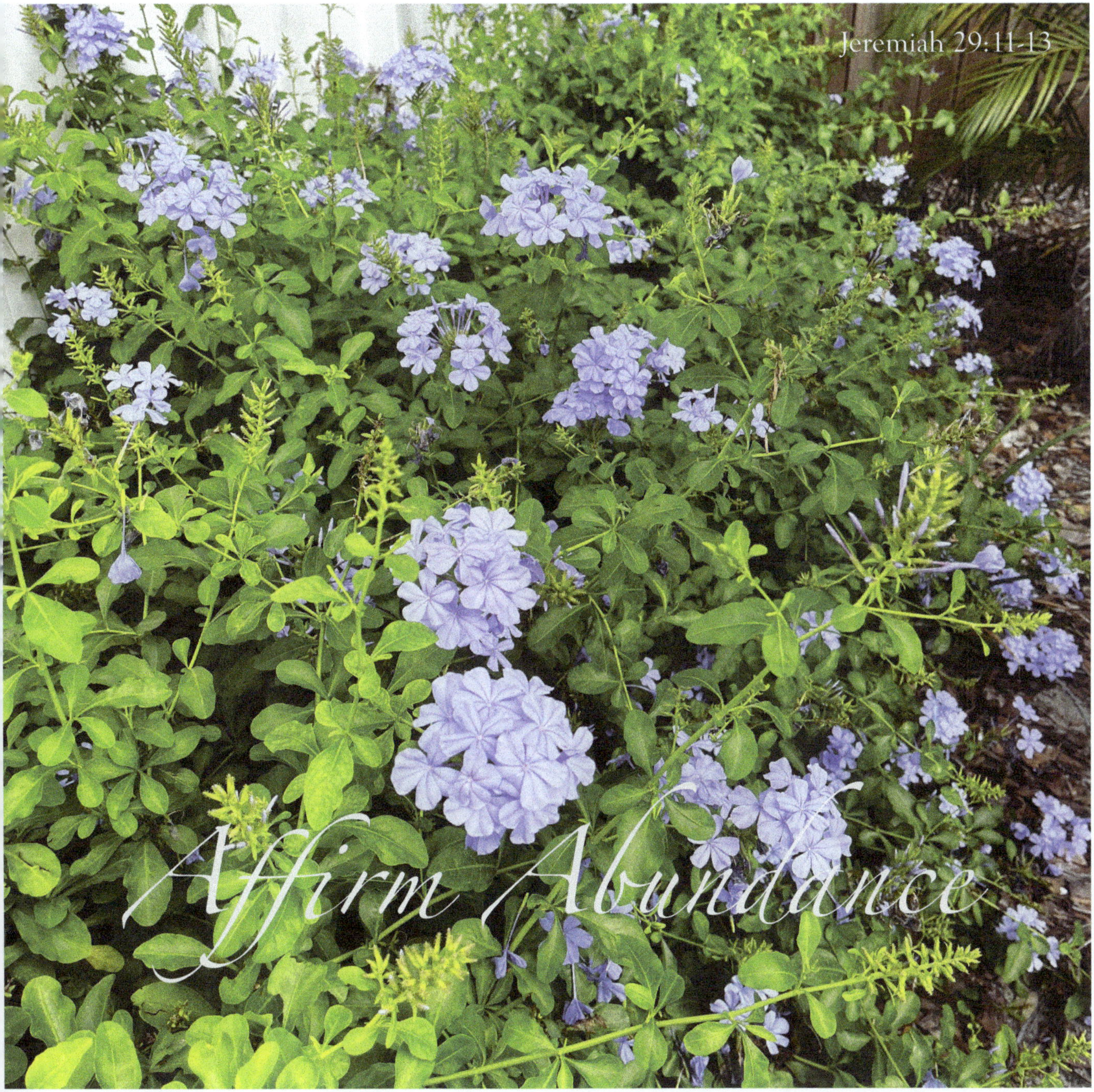
Jeremiah 29:11-13
Affirm Abundance

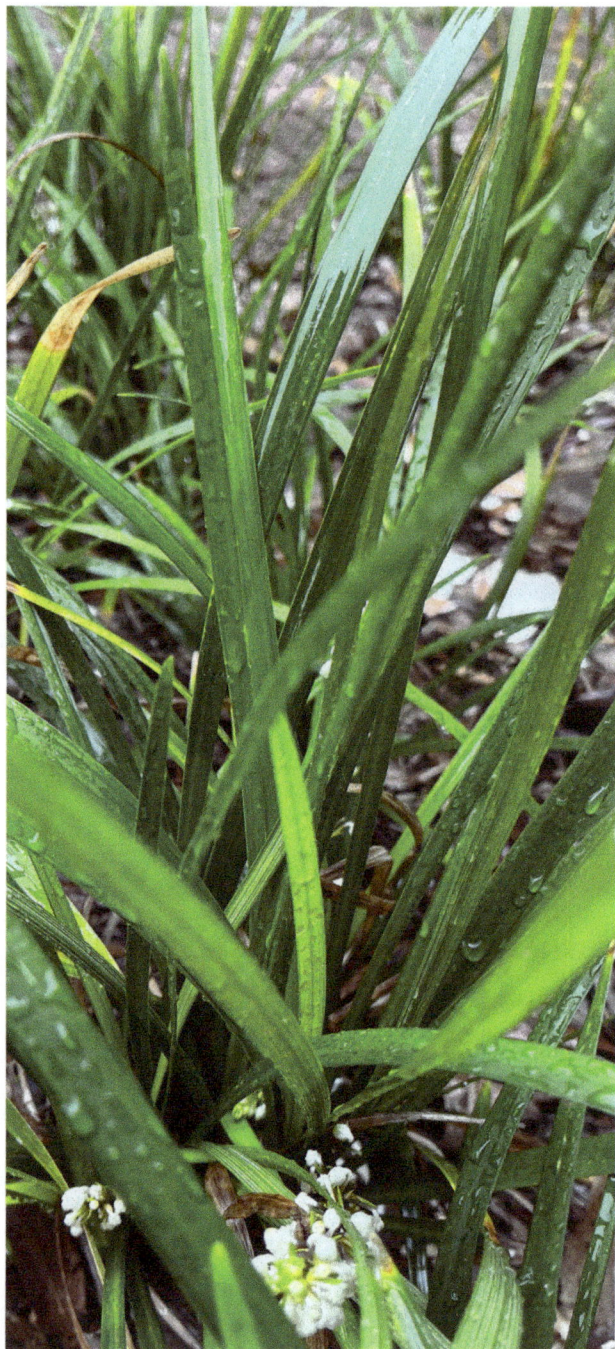

"Balance
duty and
Beauty."

Show Appreciation

Cat let out a sigh, a little flustered by the under-current of disharmony around her. She fluttered to the ground to rest. As she got closer, she noticed white and lilac blooms tucked inside of graceful long leaves.

"You have such lovely blooms for grass," complimented Cat.

"Really? We never get compliments. And we aren't grass," huffed Liriope.

"We are perfunctory border plants, barely noticed at all. We define the borders for the other plants and other mundane tasks," muttered the Liriope.

"You do bloom. You also provide structure and order to Picket. You provide useful services so you are very important and quite attractive, too. You are both," pointed out Cat.

"I suppose we do add Beauty. One can get so busy with work, work, work, that we forget about Beauty," nodded Liriope as he stood a little straighter.

"Balance duty with Beauty. Duty then Beauty then duty then Beauty," suggested Cat.

"After The Great Sinking Scare, many of us got trampled and discarded. It was an uncertain era. The land was starting to give way below us. We dropped several inches and feared we would drop more. We were incredibly insecure. In an instant, Picket could have disappeared altogether into a big lake. It's not uncommon for acquifers and sand to shift. Thankfully Picket stabalized. We all got moved around after the scare only for our usefulness to hold soil in place and direct water flow. Beauty was not of value in that time of crisis, even though it is a core value of Picket. Beauty seemed broken. The Great Sinking Scare changed our perceptions for those of us who were in Picket at the time. We focused only on the problem at hand. I guess I simply forgot about Beauty," explained Liriope.

"Remember your Beauty. You are valuable. Thank you for your service. You are so very appreciated and admired," said Cat.

She looked down the neat line of Liriope all listening, and they each stood a little taller and pushed up their white and lilac blooms so Cat could admire them, too.

Photo: Lilyturf, Liriope Muscari

Be Fruitful

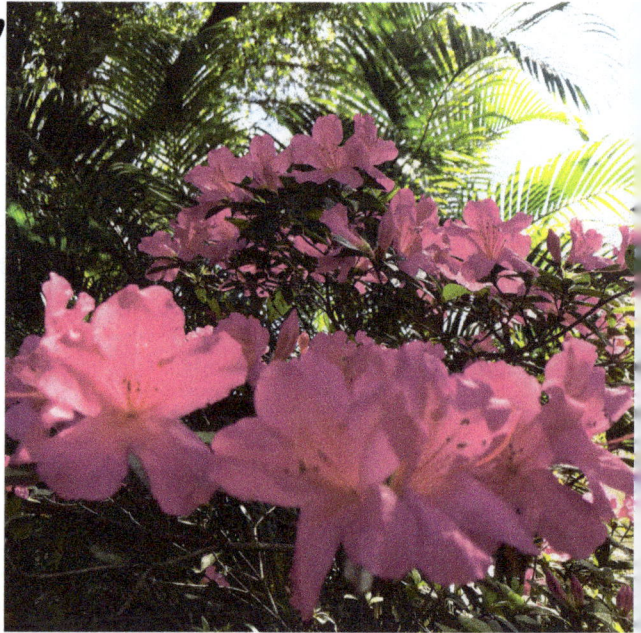

A bibelot caught the attention of Cat.

Azalea was dangling a trinket-sized fuchsia bud from a branch. The decorative ornament captivated her.

"Come enjoy my buds and my blooms," invited Azalea.

Cat fluttered over to the tallest plant she had visited so far.

"Wow! I can see forever from here!" exclaimed Cat.

"I've been here forever so I've had a lot of time to grow," laughed Azalea.

"I've bordered Picket since the time of the start of The Great Oak era. We were close friends for many, many decades, and our ancestors before us for many centuries. There are many Azaleas around Picket but I am by far the eldest, and some say wisest. I thought I would further explain the seeming uneasiness of the plants as told by Liriope," he offered.

"Do tell me. I would like to be helpful if I may," said Cat listening intently.

"During The Great Sinking Scare, many plants did get trampled and removed. Also, many tall plants and trees got removed because their deep, expansive roots were thought to be problematic and a cause of sinking. It truly was a time of incredible apprehension and ferocious fear. We questioned our very survival. As the cleared plots got re-planted, only edibles got space at first. Mango, Banana, Meyer Lemon and Olive Trees joined us at that time. In time, they each will grow to take up greater spaces. Around them, Tomato and Pepper Plants joined us. So, some plants of the The Great Sinking Scare time period try with great fervor to show usefulness. A rumor was that many of us in time will be replaced with edibles and fruit-bearers. It is feared that our once pristine ornamental formal garden may become a practical functional garden. The transition has started. We are losing our long-held identity. The Fall of The Great Oak further deteriorated our sense of self and security. Our continuity of daily life changed dramatically.

The Sun has been brutally harsh on us. Now we are in a season of re-set with nervous botanicals vying for attention, prestige and power. We lack proper leadership and power. The very essence of Picket is shifting," Azalea advised.

"I'm worried for all of my new friends. Can't Picket be both ornamental and functional?" asked Cat.

"Life is full of choices. There is only so much time and space and resources. For you Butterflies to live in Picket, Milkweed grows for the Caterpillars. Picket has to value the Beauty of Butterflies to plant the not so attractive, nor edible Milkweed," said Azalea.

"Now I'm also concerned for myself and the future Butterflies in Picket," shuddered Cat.

Azalea and Cat both sat quietly for a few moments. Cat was learning about life in Picket. Cat was learning about life in general. Beauty was just the beginning.

"You can be aware of potential adversities and obstacles and not harbor fear. Do the best you can daily to contribute to solutions. You can't be a part of a solution if you don't even know what the problem is. Don't ignore problems. Enlighten and educate yourself. Every place and every group through all of time experiences issues. The goal is to minimize threats and harm to yourself and others. Be the best that you can be as an individual. Work hard. Bear your variety of fruit as you wish. Flowers love the freedom to be fruitful," said Azalea.

"I remember one time when I was heavy-hearted and The Sky told me, 'So, do your work as birds have done, And I will do the rest.' My work is to communicate as a social butterfly. I'll flit and float and inform the others that they are both fruitful and beautiful. I'll encourage the most vibrant of colors in my botanical buddies," announced Cat.

Photo: Azaleas, Rhododendron

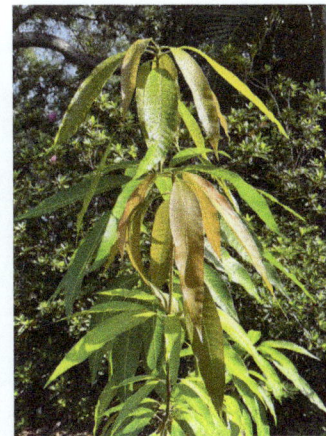

Photo: Meyer Lemon Tree, Banana Tree, Olive Tree or Olea Europaea, Mango Tree

Protect Each Other

"Avoid Word Warfare."

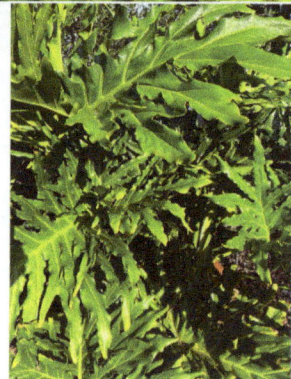

Cat continued her explorations. She noticed mature ferns in big clumps, and smaller ferns bravely branching out under The Sun.

"Good morning! What are you chatting about all huddled together?" asked Cat.

"We had to gather closely to protect each other after the Fall of The Great Oak," explained the Ferns.

"The young ones adapt to change more easily. They bravely venture out into the sunny spots and thrive. The young will do fine. They didn't know The Great Oak and our previous way of life. Daily life was much easier when we had shade, stucture and protection," said an older Fern.

A Coontie nearby teased, "Some say you Ferns are Weeds."

"That's not nice to say to the Ferns," scolded Cat.

"I'm just teasing them. Actually, I am making fun of myself because I am Fern-like and Palm-like, too. I am a Cycad," said the large green sphere Coontie.

"I am much larger so I can take the teasing. I'm not easily intimidated. My massive friend right over there, Philodendron, picks on me constantly. I poke him back, and we go around-and-around. He makes me laugh. Humor makes the long summer days pass with pleasure. We don't say anything mean, just funny. Still, the teasing can be hurtful to the sensitive ones. So, for example, I don't tease Aloe because they don't see the humor in our banter. They don't have the advantage of being near to us physically, so we cannot caress them and assure them we are friendly and safe. We converse with them all of the time, but we leave the humor to our inner circle. Not all plants are as considerate of others' feelings. Some really are mean-spirited. We avoid those who intentionally harm others. Some enjoy word warfare but it's best to avoid word warfare because it starts ... war," the gentleman said not identifying the mean ones.

"Our past civility and innate kindness eroded with the Fall of The Great Oak. We are in a new era of edginess. Now sarcasm has replaced compassion. All the plants pick on one another incessantly. It's like they are grasping for power, but will never have power like The Great Oak. In our plot, I actually am larger and stronger, and the Ferns know that I adore them. They protect each other huddled together and I protect them by shading my smaller neighbors. We all watch out for each other. We are like family," Coontie said.

"You protect them. You adore them. Do you love them?" curiously asked Cat.

"Not romantic love, but love of fellows is steadfast in Picket. Love is the root of everything in Picket. We understand that Beauty is enhanced by Love. Love nurtures Beauty. They go hand-in-hand," remarked Coontie.

Photo: Coontie, Zamia Integrifolia
Boston Fern or Sword Fern, Nephrolepis Exaltata
Aloe, Aloe Barbadensis Miller
Philodendron Xanadu, Thaumatophyllum Xanadu

Use Your Manners

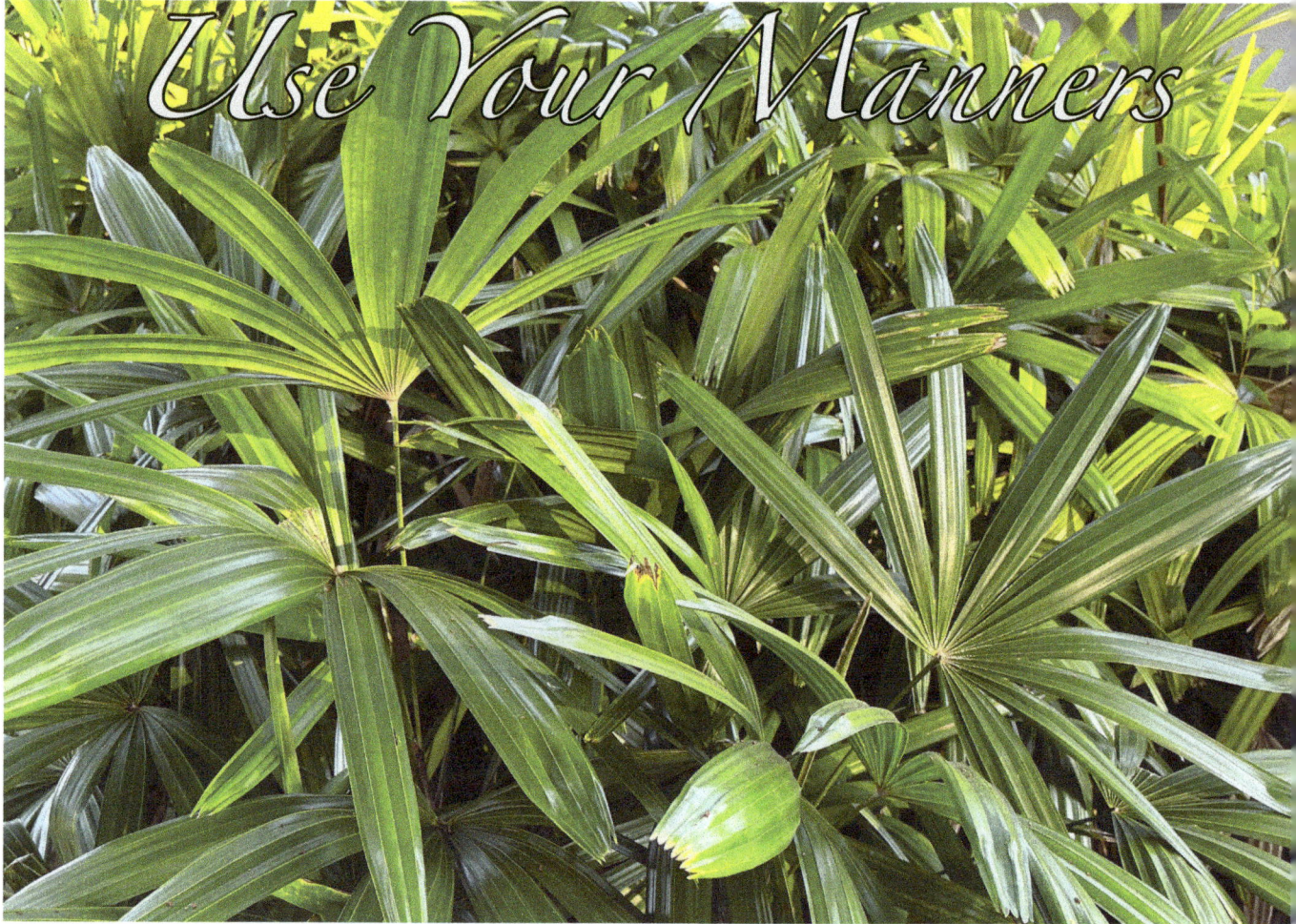

Cat heard a murmur and was drawn to a hedge of Lady Palms behind the Coontie and Ferns.

"Lady Palms! You are so majestically astonishing," said Cat as she floated over to the erudite hedge admiring their elegant stature.

"We were highly favored by The Great Oak. Several of the Oaks fell during The Great Wind Catastrophes. We Lady Palms take a long time to grow just like the Oaks. We are loyal and we set our roots deep. We cannot just up and move on a whim. So here we sit under a scorching sun," complained Lady Palm.

"You still exude grand Beauty," said Cat.

"We won't maintain our current Beauty for long. Our leaves have gone from emerald green to yellow and next they will turn brown and fall off of us. It will take decades to recover from our singed leaves," complained the pampered Lady Palm.

"Why don't you drop the browning leaves and keep just the green ones?" asked Cat.

"Do not the brown ones still give shade? We are covering our young with the pains of our past. Knowing of our past misfortunes helps our future Lady Palms learn about our hardships and how to overcome them. We were among the first in Picket and now to appease the newcomers, we have sunshine everywhere. Who needs all this light? It's been devastating. We are sturdy and will recover in time, but it won't be easy. We liked the formal garden design. Why did it have to change? What good did all the changes do?" asked Lady Palm.

"I'm sure The Great Oak didn't abandon you intentionally. If you forgive and accept, it can help heal you," said Cat.

"Our Le Jardin was a manicured garden before the Fall of The Great Oak. Now everything is just willynilly. I'll never forgive him for leaving us in this dire predicament. We don't want to be around all the sun-loving plants. The new plants brush right up against us and spread their seeds all over our plot. Just look at how Nandina shoots over roots to pop up new plants right next to us. They are just like Weeds! They were not invited. They are pushy and rude. They have no manners or social graces. The African Iris were the pushiest. Their blooms are simply divine but they clump and their roots grow too tightly and deeply into the soil that they choke all plants around them. They even choke themselves. Most of them got taken out of Picket Park Place with a few sequestered ones left. Now, understand that we accept some new plants. We made peace with the Areca Palms years ago. They pushed us over a little then stayed clumped in the corners. They have grown incredibly high, so we now appreciate their magnificent shade. They are actually quite good neighbors," spoke up one punctilious Lady Palm.

"Maybe the other new plants you will find useful and neighborly in time. Give them a chance. Set an example. You want the new plants to have social graces and manners, so shouldn't you be likewise gracious to them?" innocently asked Cat.

"Why heavens no. This is our plot for generations. We live here the way we always have. We get to choose with whom we socialize with in Picket," said Lady Palm.

Cat felt a little defensive. She technically was new, too.

"Things have changed around you. Everything is different it seems. All the plants, whether old or new, are dissatisfied or uncomfortable about one thing or another. If you ask nicely, maybe the new plants will respect your boundaries and traditions. Do they even know your traditions? Maybe you can teach them the history of Picket like you are teaching your little ones. If each plant shared their perspectives on the past and visons for the future, then agreements could be made for the present. Everyone wants the same thing. We all strive for Beauty. I think if all plants used their manners, then all the other plants would respond kindly. United, we can create more Beauty. Harmony could help," pondered Cat.

Photo: Lady Palms or Rhaphis Palms, Rhapis Excelsa

"United we can create more Beauty."

Photo: Nandina or Heavenly Bamboo, Nandina Domestica
Areca Palm or Bamboo Palm or Golden Cane Palm, Dypsis lutescens
African Iris or Fortnight Lily, Dietes Iridioides

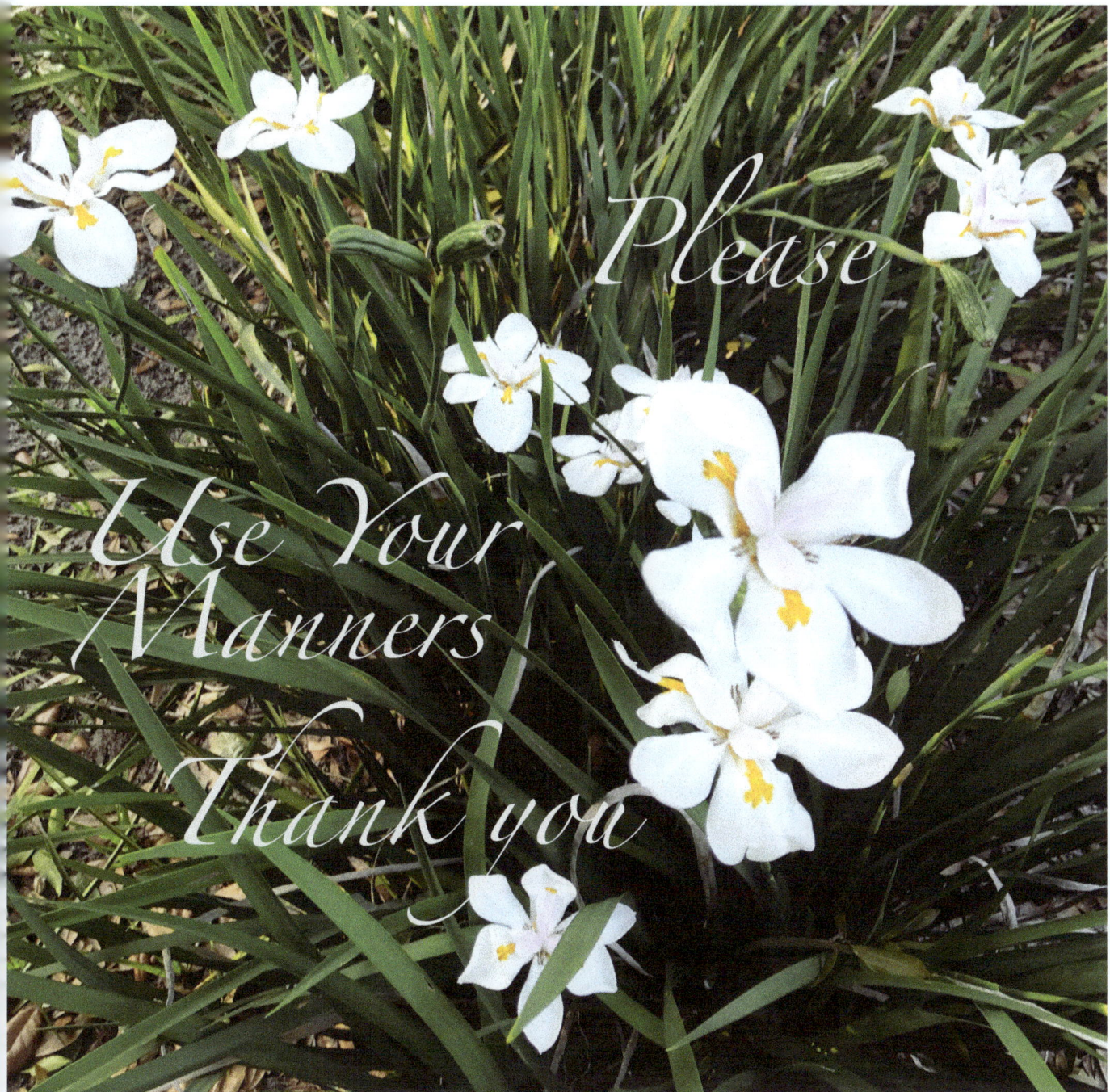

An alluring flowering bush chimed in to the conversation.

"My mother always told me you can't learn how to have class, you have to be born with it. True Beauty is much the same," declared Camellia, the tallest of all the Pinks in Picket.

"All the talk of Beauty around Picket is tacky and sophomoric. The plants of Picket are obsessed with Beauty but they don't understand it. True Beauty simply exists. It doesn't have to be explained, just experienced. We Camellias bloom each fall to spring to set a solid example and inspire the others to bloom. We remind the botanicals of intrinsic true Beauty that is in all of us," explained Camellia.

"I want to know true Beauty. You are so very beautiful. You have so many blooms. You have golden crowns caressed inside your royal pink silky petals," admired Cat.

"You are observant. Rarely do others take note of our crowns. Perhaps we knew of each other in a past transition. It was your spirit and not your sight that recognized a royal line. Our lineage goes far back in history. The era of a royal nature has long passed. A verifiable essence, however, does not pass. What is inside of you stays with you forever. If you had once been a princess, you are forever a princess in the way you see the world throughout the ages. My leadership role now is to pass on what I know about Beauty in the world. I am here in this lifetime to remind the flowers that they are loved by The Sky," said Camellia.

Cat found her a tad haughty but she was enchanted by Camellia and yearned to learn more. This could be her mentor, her teacher, for assisting her in her quest to fly to The Sky.

"What can I do to help bring more Beauty back to Picket?" asked Cat.

"Picket Park Place was one of the most prosperous places for a vast variety of blooms. We were guided by the Picket Principle of The Dream. The Great Oak was a shining example of living The Dream. The Picket Principle was for each plant to envision the best that it could be and then go be it. We had total freedom which enabled each individual plant to work hard and look for opportunities to be as beautiful as possible. It worked. Picket was a dreamy place in a magical space in time," said Camellia.

"You are talking about Picket as though we are in the past ...," questioned a confused Cat.

"We are at a time of a turning point. Plants of Picket are making choices, and at the same time, choices are being made for us. Our past is only our future if we understand it, value it, cherish it and choose it. We have to all choose it together. That takes leadership," said Camilla.

"Can you teach others to lead as you do? I know that Pinwheel Jasmine wants higher-thinking companions. He sees himself as a leader," offered Cat.

"He is perhaps a future leader. He is a leader in training. He may, however, never be a leader. Many leaders fall due to false premises. He senses himself as superior to the little Pinks. He is not. It is his role now to live among them to understand them and be devoted to them. Until he loves the plants of Picket more than himself, he cannot be a leader of them. Leaders without love fail," Camellia explained.

There was that love word again Cat noted. She also noted it was not romantic love being discussed. She deeply craved to fully understand the promises of The Sky. She especially wished for romantic love.

Lead with Love

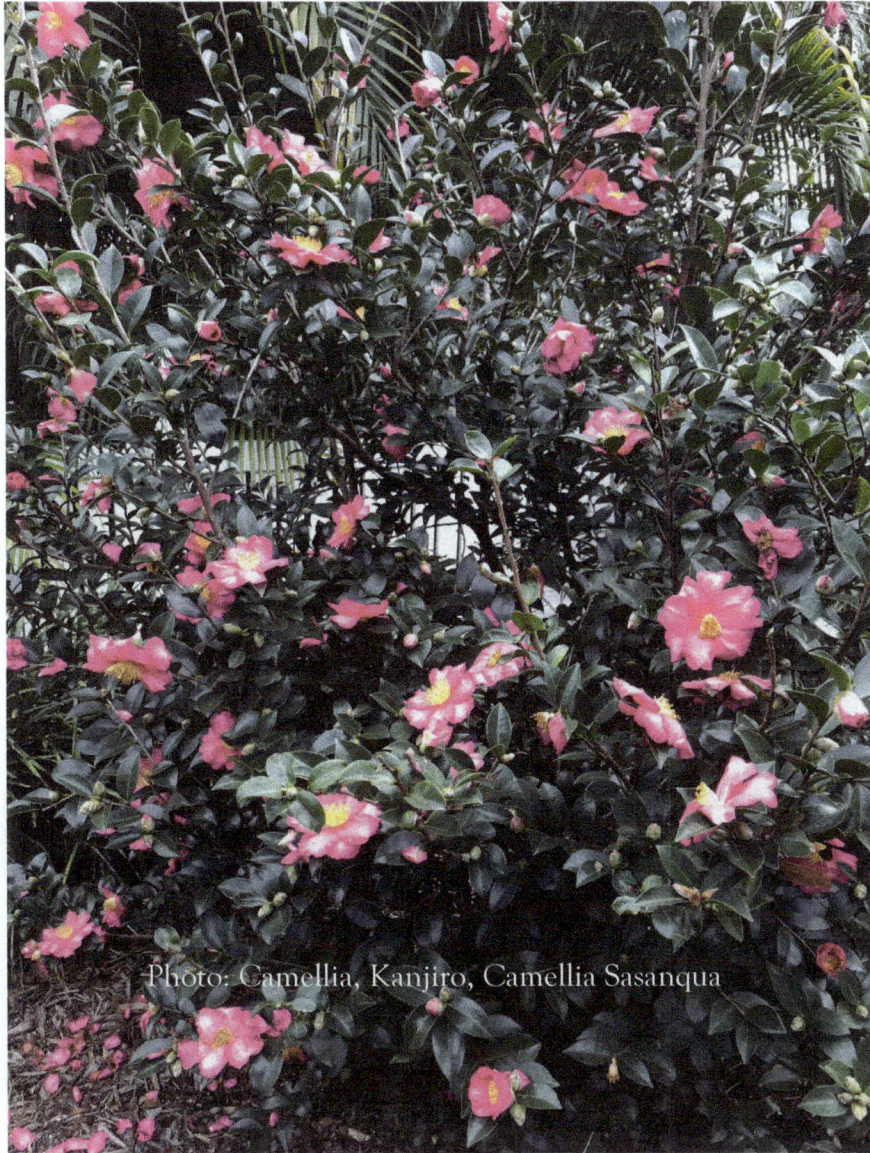

Photo: Camellia, Kanjiro, Camellia Sasanqua

Photo: Gardenia, Gardenia Jasminoides

Make Peace Within Yourself

A fantastic fragrance bathed Cat as she turned to hear another voice.

"When Camellias stop blooming, we Gardenias take over spring through summer so the statuesque bushes in Picket bloom year-round," nodded Gardenia.

"We have a long history here, too. We are the anchor plants and offer advice to all the newcomers and smaller plants. We keep the peace in Picket," said the elegant elder Gardenia.

"So, you have peace? I'm looking for peace. The Sky told me I would find Peace and Joy and Love here in Picket," said Cat excitedly.

"You don't find peace like a treasure chest," laughed Gardenia, "You create peace within yourself by accepting what is and what is not."

"So, like some others here, you are not concerned with The Great Sinking Scare, The Great Wind Catastrophes, The Fall of The Great Oak, sun and shade, change and moving ..." asked Cat.

"I accept my surroundings. I accept those around me. I accept myself exactly as I am. My peace is not to be found; it exists within me. Peace already exists within you, too," said Gardenia.

"I've been listening so much to worry and concern of the others, I fear I have taken some of their burdens onto my own wings. Also, I know I have limited time in Picket, as we all do, so I want to fulfill The Sky's promise to find Peace and Joy and Love," poured out Cat.

"You are fluttering around and finding yourself. You have to find yourself first. You've had wings for a short time. Life is a process to be enjoyed. You are finding yourself as a reflection off of the others. You were meant to meet them. You cannot easily find these things you seek. You may never possess all three at the same time. If you do, you will be one of the very lucky ones. That doesn't mean that The Sky's promise will not be fulfilled, but it may look differently than what you imagined," clarified Gardenia.

"When I was quiet after my time as a Caterpillar before I was a Butterfly I listened intently to my inner voice. I heard The Sky very specifically tell me I would have Peace and Joy and Love. I believe I will experience all three at the same time," said Cat.

"Only you and The Sky know your destiny. Like attracts like. So make peace within yourself and that will help you attract others who are at peace," Gardenia suggested.

Communicate Clearly and Honestly

After meeting so many new plants, Cat longed for the familiar. Since she had become a Butterfly, everything was so fresh and stimulating. She was realizing she had so very much to learn. She floated back to the Caterpillar Corner. To her great delight, a Butterfly popped out from behind an iris. A handful of Butterflies floated all around her.

"Hello. I'm Cat and I was a caterpillar here, too," greeted Cat.

"We know," growled an orange Butterfly.

"We heard already about you," jabbed another Butterfly with a smirk.

"Why, I don't understand. We are so similar. We are in the same family of Butterflies even. I can tell by your colors and markings that we are more similar than different. We should be friendly," she suggested.

The pretentious ones ignored her.

"What negative thing could you possibly hear and from whom?" Cat questioned completely shocked by their unexpectedly rude behavior.

"We no longer value social Butterflies with their old-fashioned way of communicating. Purple Heart tells us everything about everyone in Picket," snipped Butterfly.

"Well, if Purple Heart told you something about me, it must not be true. I don't even know a plant by that name and I've done nothing to harm anything in my time in Picket. To resolve conflict and misunderstanding, why don't you tell me what it is that you heard and give me a chance to tell you my perspective on the topic. You hear them, so now hear my side. Let's communicate clearly and honestly," suggested Cat, trying to be practical and not give in to her increasingly hurt feelings.

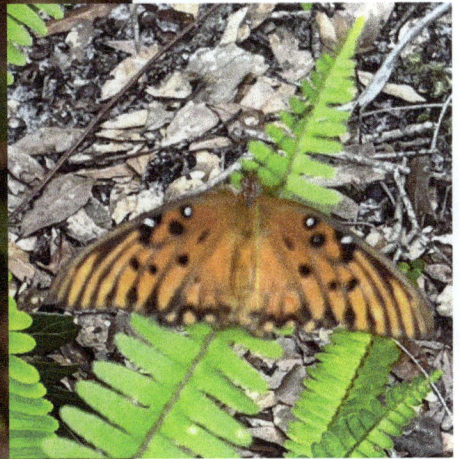

Photo: Passion Butterfly or Gulf Fritillary (Linnaeus), Dione Vanillae,
similar to Monarchs in the family of Nymphalidae Brush-Footed Butterflies

Find Tranquility in Troubles

An elder Lady Palm called Cat over to her and spoke so all of Caterpillar Corner could hear.

"Understand that it's not that the Purple Hearts don't like you, it's that you annoy and irritate them because of your natural Beauty, which is the inside Beauty of a pure heart. They have a Purple Heart. You have a pure heart. Many plants have forgotten about inner Beauty. Others have given up on sharing how to grow within, and stick to their like-minded peers who already possess the knowledge. Many plants are misguided now and are fixated on appearance in such a way that the very essence of Beauty eludes them.

They want to appear to be useful or powerful or intelligent or visually pleasing. Appearances alone do not make a lovely flower," said Lady Palm.

"So, because I understand Beauty they are attacking me?" asked a confused and increasingly annoyed Cat.

"Purple Hearts have no heart at all. Even their name is misleading. They are the most hateful of all of Picket. They are what my mother called "Little People." They are the wannabes who are fueled by jealousy. They are the gossips, busy-bodies and trouble makers. They are more physically attractive than Weeds, in fact, quite ornamental some say, but inside they share the traits of Weeds as takers and opportunists. They have charisma and charm and weasel their way in among the plants. The cons blend well among the flowers visually, so they ingratiate themselves into social circles under false pretenses. They are the ultimate pretenders and fakes with dangerous grand aspirations," said Lady Palm.

"Please point them out to me so I can avoid them," begged Cat.

"You have passed by them all day. They are hiding in plain sight. Like Weeds, they spread easily. They keep shallow roots so they can sneakily move around to create mischief with their fabrications, exaggerations, accusations and outright lies. They spread rumors to incite difficulties and hardships for others. They delight in the chaos and destruction caused by their plotting. Their greedy, corrupt insatiable cravings and extreme arrogance will lead them to their ultimate demise. The Sky foretold of the extinction of their line. They will perish forever," said Lady Palm.

"In the meantime, what am I to do? Should I confront the Purple Hearts? Should I try to engage the snarky Butterflies again?" asked Cat.

"Evil intentions evaporate. Truth lasts forever. Good overcomes the wicked. Do not concern yourself with the iniquity of the morally corrupt. Giving it attention gives it power over you. Focusing on their undeserved attacks will distract you from your many blessings. Keep your energy pure and your power focused on your own heart's desire as promised by The Sky," said Lady Palm.

"Picket is not as agreeable and cohesive as I had imagined as a Caterpillar. I did not realize I would be slandered and betrayed. I am shocked and hurt," said Cat.

"Do not be dismayed. Liars attack many unsuspecting ones. Only the weak or morally feeble listen to them because they do have the mind to know better. Those Butterflies were new to Picket so they were vulnerable to the conniving of vindictive ones. They will get a taste of their wicked ways in time. The traitors will turn on their unsuspecting supporters, too. Find tranquility in your troubles. Be at peace about yourself knowing they are not in Truth," said Lady Palm.

"I thought this would be easier. So, through trouble and strife I am to learn of peace?" asked Cat.

"A brush with strife makes you stronger. To know what is not peaceful indeed affirms when peace is present," advised Lady Palm.

Photo: Purple Queen or Purple Heart, Tradescantia Pallida

Cherish Your Freedoms

A Gardenia offered intercession.

"Flowers, like Butterflies, are delicate and not suitable for such significant strife. Take heart. You are not alone in this. We as a garden need to regain the peace that comes with freedom for flowers," stated the soft-spoken young adult Gardenia.

"Many are trapped in worry, anger and angst causing them to act in abnormally aggressive and desperate ways. They do not feel the gift of freedom. The misguided plants are simply reacting, but not with logic or beneficial outcomes. They don't fully comprehend what they cannot control, that which is thrust upon them in a manipulative manner, so they started trying to control the world around them. They began picking on each other and picking sides causing divisiveness. Previously we would aspire to higher thoughts such as Peace and Joy and Love as you seek. Their mental and emotional separation from each other will lure more of The Great Catastrophes. With rampant preoccupation of the recent chaos, starting with The Great Sinking Scare, The Great Wind Catastrophes and the Fall of The Great Oak, we started losing our freedoms. Our thoughts were filled with fear and not Beauty. Persistent fear paralyzes progress with mental and emotional bondage. Lack of freedom is not always of a physical nature. While we stared at fear in front of us, freedoms dripped away behind us. We need freedom from fear and from real or perceived oppression for the survival of our society," he pontificated.

"The distractions of fear caused the flowers to start giving up their freedoms?" asked Cat.

"Fear is a theif of time and energy. Picket has been prosperous and powerful because free flowers love the opportunity to aspire to, achieve and possess the highest level of Beauty. That takes a work ethic of free flowers. It also takes free time to dream. Liberty affords the luxury of leisure. We are losing the coveted freedoms of time and attention to devote to our individual heart's desires, dreams and life purposes. This is causing spiritual stagnation and pausing our souls' purposes. Furthermore, it blocks our blessings," he continued.

"Those are very astute observations. Life in Picket is predicated upon our freedoms," said Cat as she pondered his wisdom.

He was free to discuss with her his philosophy. She was free to listen. She listened well. The two new friends bonded quickly.

Photo: Gardenia, Gardenia Jasminoides

"Liberty affords the luxury of leisure."

Grow Guidance

Cat bounced back to one of the Camellias.

"Now I am starting to feel insecure like some of the others. I am questioning my purpose here in Picket. I dreamed to fly as high as The Sky. I was seeking the secrets to Peace and Joy and Love as promised to me by The Sky. Instead I have connected with discontent, superficiality, superiority, fear, jealousy, back-stabbing, competitiveness, edginess, cynicism and outright meanness. I can't un-see or un-hear the garden griping and gossip. How am I to find the things I seek of a higher nature among the hardened hearts?" asked Cat.

"Now you sound negative yourself. Watch your words. Words have power. Focusing on negativity blocks and on positivity opens. The plants weren't all hardened. You had lovely interactions. Some shared joy with you. You soothed and comforted some with your unique perspectives, gentle words and natural grace. Like your wings, your words are fluttering among them. You expected to flit around and have happiness and success come effortlessly and quickly. Expectations can fuel our disappointments," said Camellia.

"I'll change my words. I can do that. What should I expect now?" asked Cat.

"From what I see, you have become proficient in sincere Beauty. That is what we learn here in Picket. You have not once mentioned your own Beauty. That is because you have already learned that inner Beauty is what is to be treasured. It is sensed and not seen. Why don't you ask The Sky? Maybe you have mastered all you can learn in Picket to get closer to your heart's desire. Maybe it is time for you to transition again," advised Camellia.

"Gardenia was just speaking of freedom. I am free to change. I am not stifled for any reason at all ... but I just got here! Transition to what now? Where am I to go? What am I to do? How will I know?" asked Cat.

"How did you know to come to Picket? How did you get here? How did you assess who to trust? You came here to grow your guidance in the garden. You have been listening to the earthly world around you but not listening inward or looking upward to The Sky. Listen again for discernment and direction. You will achieve your dream to fly to The Sky. You were promised your heart's desire for Peace and Joy and Love. Now show gratitude to receive your blessings," said Camellia and she paused.

"Just as some of the flowers have forgotten true inner Beauty, you have forgotten that you have wings," hinted Camellia.

Cat was excited about the proclamation being made over her by Camellia.

"I've been so busy socializing around the grounds, that I have put no effort into even trying to fly to The Sky. In addition, I had not considered at all that my heart's desire was not actually located in Picket. I had limited my search to only the familiar. I am so grateful for my wings! I could fly anywhere, just anywhere," Cat marveled.

Photo: Camellia, Kanjiro, Camellia Sasanqua

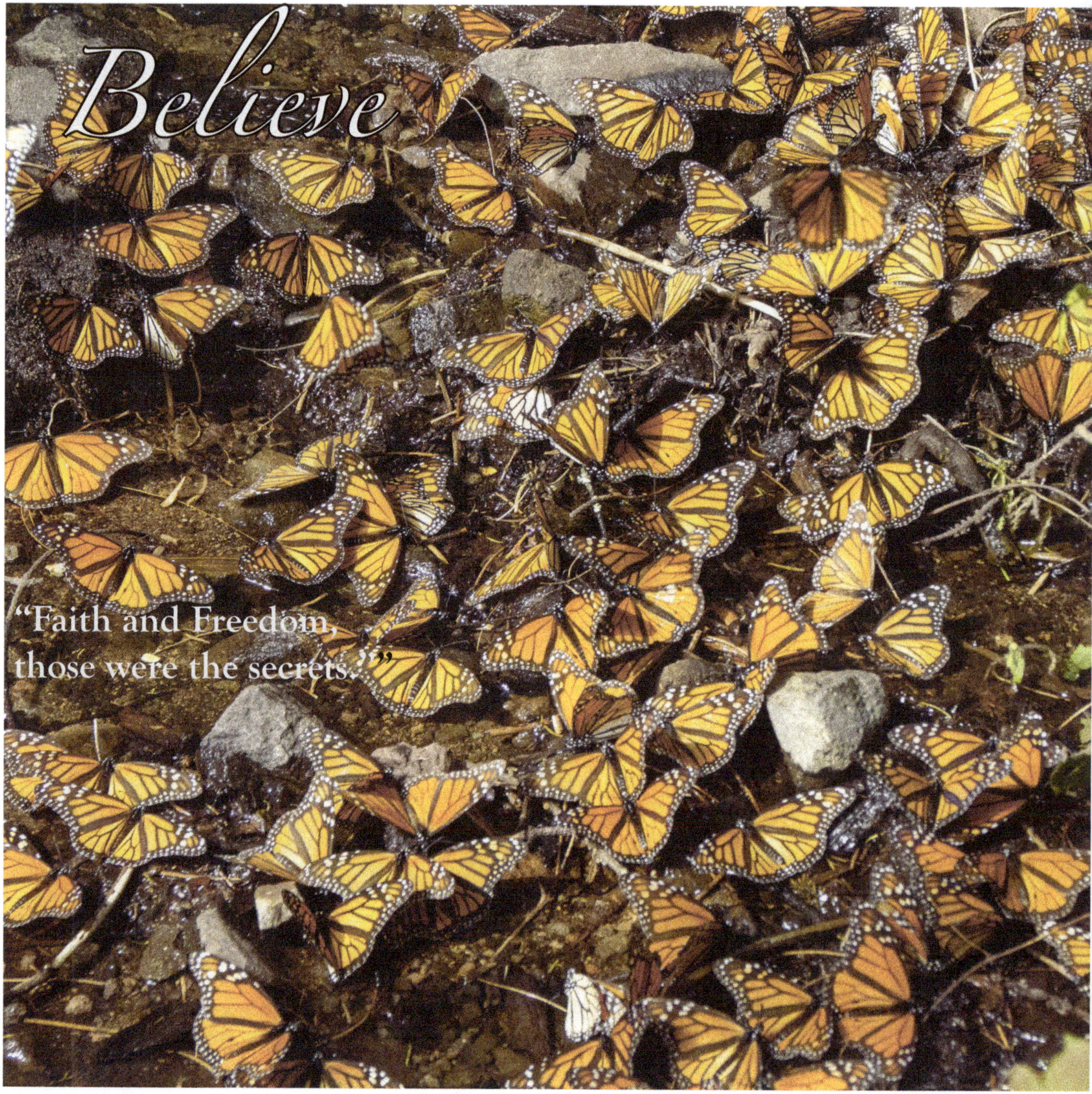
Believe
"Faith and Freedom,
those were the secrets."

"Be still. Have courage to create your dream and receive your promise," suggested Camellia.

Camilla sat with her quietly. They were still for a spell.

Cat then felt a strong serene yet stimulating sensation. She was given a vision of a magical multitude of Monarchs. She felt Peace and Joy and Love simultaneously just as The Sky had promised. The promise was kept. She wanted her gift to last forever.

"I am so grateful for my guidance to gift to me this sensation of Peace and Joy and Love," she exclaimed.

The quiddity of an incoming sound was distinctively Monarch wings. She then looked up to witness her promise come true. She didn't know this group was her heart's desire until she saw the sky filled with fluttering. She saw what was to be her current day family, friends, sincere supporters and even a soulmate for this lifetime both above her and joining her on the ground. She knew in an instant her heart's desire was fulfilled as promised. The Monarch community would connect her to Peace and Joy and Love. From over the picket fence, delicate tangerine colored wings flapped as far as she could see up to The Sky. They were guiding her to where they lived high in the giant trees near Picket. She would live so much closer to The Sky. Her worldly dream was to fly to The Sky and now she didn't have to fly as far, or fly alone. Cat found what she was looking for in Picket, but it wasn't physically there. The lessons were there not the destiny. Her true heart's desire was to be found in her next transition with the Monarchs near The Sky.

Cat was elated. Her wings waved goodbye to her botanical friends in Picket Park Place. She was not leaving them forever. She would always be a part of them. She showed them to hold tightly to their foundational beliefs and core values of botanical Beauty. She was setting an example to follow a dream and reminding them to follow their own dreams. Her dream was coming true. She was shining an example of The Dream of one garden under The Sky. She sprinkled renewed hope in The Dream as they watched her fly higher and higher. Not only did she feel Peace and Joy and Love herself, but she misted her spiritual gifts like fairy dust as she circled the plants of Picket. She was leading with love. She vowed she would return to visit. She loved her flower friends.

With the many Monarchs, she ascended over the serene spiritual space overflowing with flora and fauna that shared with her the secrets of Peace and Joy and Love. The secret was her unwavering belief in the promise of the Divine. Faith of the spirit fulfilled her heart's desire. Freedom of a worldly nature made The Dream possible. Faith and Freedom, those were the secrets.

You are Loved

Flow with Flowers. Look for related information online by Casey Tennyson Author & Ghostwriter.